ARMOND E MOSLEY

D1607900

God Bless

THE **5** THINGS EVERY TEEN SHOULD KNOW ABOUT SEX

MG Publishing Company

Books may be purchased in bulk quantity and/or special sales by contacting the publisher, MG Publishing Company, at MGPublishingCo@gmail.com or by phone at 484.420.6614.

Published by: MG Publishing Company
a division of Kingdom Workshops, LLC.
MGPublishingCo@gmail.com

Cover design by: Marie Morrison Designs

Interior design by: Godzchild Publications

Editing by: Godzchild Publications

Library of Congress Catalog Number: 2013914574

ISBN: 978-0-9897759-0-8

1. Abstinence 2. Teens 3. Christianity; Includes bibliographical references, and scriptural references.

Printed in the United States of America 2013 – 1st Edition

TABLE OF CONTENTS

Preface

What's Up?!

If you're reading this book right now, it means you are at a point in your life where you want to learn more about sex...or someone close to you is making you read it (lol). Either way, before we move ahead, I want to thank you for your time. I know that there are a million and one other things you could be doing with your time right now, so for you to sit and take the time to read my book is very humbling. Thank you.

So, who is this book for? It's for every teenager, 13 – 18 years old. It's for the teenager who is currently a virgin and hasn't yet had to deal with sex in his or her life. It's for the teenager who has explored sex here and there, but isn't quite sure how they feel about it yet. It's for the teenager who is sexually active, has had multiple partners, and doesn't really see the point in stopping now. Ultimately, no matter how much sexual experience you do or don't have, this book is for you.

At this point in your life, I'm sure you've not only read other books about sex, but your parents, teachers, and church leaders have all been beating you in the head with the whole, "Don't do it!" message. And for every time you've heard this message, you've heard or witnessed something at school or on TV that left you thinking to yourself, "Why not?" And that's a great question; one that by the time you finish reading this book, you will have an answer to.

You see, there are many opinions out there about sex. **When you should do it. Who you should do it with. How you should do it.** And even, **what will happen to you if you don't do it.** Have you ever heard anyone talk about these questions before? I'm sure you have and it has probably been from one of your friends or even a family member. And while I'm sure you love and trust your friends and family, the 'advice' and 'wisdom' you get from them can quickly become more confusing than helpful. That's why it is important for you to come up with your own opinions about sex so that the decisions you make will be your own and not someone else's. This book will help you do that.

Before we move on, it's important that I share a few things with you regarding the foundation for this book. First, I want you to know that I am a Christian and as a result, many of the ideas you will read in this book are based on this fact. That said, I haven't always done what I was supposed to do as a Christian. And so, a good portion of this book will focus on my own experiences and the lessons I learned from them. You won't judge me will you?

The second thing I want you to know is that God loves you very much. And there is nothing you can do to change that. *Nothing.* And because He loves you so much, He created an Instruction Book, the Bible, just for you so that you can have the most successful and fulfilling life possible. The key though, is that you have to use it in order to access all that God has for you. I had to learn that the hard way. When I tried to figure things out on my own, I felt like I never knew what to do. I would always be confused and as a result, make the wrong decisions. But, when I started reading my Instruction Book (the Bible), I began to find the answers I was looking for and I started to make the right decisions. So, when it comes to sex and what to do or not to do, how to feel or not feel, we will begin with the Bible in order to see what it has to say.

Depending on which version of the Bible you read, you will see one of two words. If you are reading from the KJV (King James Version) you will see a word called **'fornication'.** If you are reading from the NIV (New International Version) you will see a phrase called **'sexual immorality'.** Do you know what they mean? If not, don't worry because I have their definitions here:

• *Fornication* – consensual sexual intercourse between two people not married to each other.

• *Sexual Immorality* – Sexual interaction outside of God's original intent (e.g. **fornication**: outside of marriage, **homosexuality**: with same sex, **adultery**: with a married person, **pornography**: visual stimulation (magazines, internet, DVDs, etc.) **masturbation**: self-pleasure, **groping/fondling**: inappropriate, sexually motivated touching of another).

As you can see above, fornication is a 'type' of sexual immorality. When it comes specifically to what the Bible says about sex, look no further than **1 Corinthians 6:18 (NIV),**

> *"Flee sexual immorality. All other sins a person commits are outside the body, **but whoever sins sexually, sins against their own body.**"*

Did you catch that? What did the Bible say you are supposed to do with sexual immorality? Flee! Get as far away as possible from it! This means that you are to avoid **sexual immorality** at all costs. Whatever it takes, stay away from it. To put it another way, as a Christian, you are to stay away from: 1) **sex before marriage, 2) sex with the same sex, 3) sex with a married person, 4) pornography, 5) masturbation, and 6) groping/fondling.**

Can I keep it real with you for a second? Alright, cool. I have a confession to make. When I was younger, I thought that as long as I didn't *"put it in"* I was honoring God. So, what this meant was that I fondled, groped, dry-humped and everything else I could do with two hands and a tongue, because I thought they were ok to do. And what I found is that doing all this while trying not to have sex was extremely difficult, if not impossible. I was playing with fire and for some reason, I couldn't figure out why I kept "falling" or "slipping" back into being sexually active. But then, I came to realize (after reading the Instruction Book more and more) that all those other things were just as wrong in God's eyes because they were still "sins against my own body." They were "sins against my own body" because they brought me physical pleasure in a way that was supposed to be off-limits until marriage. As a result, I learned that ***to truly flee from sexual immorality, I had to flee from all those other things as well*** until the right time...ultimately, in marriage...with my wife.

But, enough about me. As you turn the pages, you'll have more than enough opportunities to hear more of my embarrassing stories...lol. This book will be a quick read. I encourage you to talk about what you read with your friends and if you're comfortable enough, your family. Each chapter is sure to be a conversation starter and I believe some of the biggest lessons will come from your discussions with others. So, sit back, relax, and prepare to learn The ***5 Things Every Teen Should Know About Sex.*** Enjoy!

A Special Note:
It's Never Too Late

Before you move on with this book, I want to take a moment to share something very important with you. I remember right after the first time I had sex, a part of me felt that because I had disobeyed God once, there was no point in trying to do the right thing after. I questioned whether or not God still loved me because I had done wrong. I wasn't sure if He would ever look at me in the same way He looked at those people who were still virgins; those who were able to control their sexual desires and urges and remain sexually pure. I felt dirty, filthy, and unfit to be called a child of God.

But, I was wrong. And this thinking almost made me give up my belief in who God really is. You see, God loves us...you, unconditionally. There isn't anything you can do to make Him turn His back on you. He's much more forgiving than your parents (sorry mom and dad). He's much more patient than your church leaders. He has thicker skin than your teachers, so He can take whatever you give Him. At the end of the day, He loves you more than anyone could ever love you, including yourself.

So, right now, in this moment, I want you to forget about what you may have done in the past. I don't care if you have had multiple sexual partners already or none at all. I want you to believe that your tomorrow can be better than your yesterday. It doesn't matter how many mistakes you made last year or even last week, today is a new day... the present. It's never too late to change. God welcomes change. I'm a living example of someone who made mistakes, but did not allow those mistakes to define me. If I had, I would have never changed my way of living and became celibate until marriage. Some of my friends thought I couldn't change. Some of my ex-girlfriends thought I was tripping when I wanted to change. But, you know what? None of that mattered because I wanted to change and with God's help, I was able to. And just like He did it for me, He can do the same for you. It's never too late. Today can be the first day of change for you.

Introduction:
My Story

I didn't understand it. I mean, everyone else talked about it as if it was the best feeling ever. Don't get me wrong...it did feel good, but I felt bad. See, before I had done it, I thought that when it was over I would feel like a man and even better, be "the man." But, that's not what happened. No, not at all. I felt horrible. I felt guilty. I felt shameful. I felt empty. I knew I wasn't supposed to do it, but I just had to try it. I had to make sure my boys wouldn't look at me like I was lame anymore because I was still a virgin. I had to make sure that the girls would see me as "experienced" in the bedroom and as a result, they would add me to their list of boys they wanted to get with. I had extremely high hopes of what life would be like for me when I was no longer a virgin, but those hopes were quickly shattered no sooner than I put back on my clothes.

The room was quiet as I observed tears rolling down her face. I wasn't sure why she was crying, but I as- sumed it because of the pain of her first experience. While she struggled through her emotions, I silently wrestled with my own. Why was I feeling this way? No one I knew had ever spoken of feeling guilty or shameful after having sex. What was going on with me?! As I continued to try to figure it out, all of sudden, out of nowhere, I felt the presence of someone else in the room. At first, I wasn't sure who or what it was. A ghost, maybe? Nah. My girlfriend's mother? Nope. Was it...God? No way! It was God! Wow... and that explained why I was feeling so weird. As a Christian, as His child, I had disappointed Him and I knew it.

****

Those were the emotions and feelings I had right after the first time I had sex. I remember the day clearly. It was in the spring of the year, a few weeks after I had graduated from high school. I had driven over to my girlfriend's house to "take our relationship to the next level." It was premeditated. We had discussed it for weeks. She was a virgin. I was too...but, she didn't know that. I lied to her so that she would think I knew what to do. So, when I got to her house we put our plan into effect. But, something was off from the beginning. It didn't feel "right" and when it was over, I quickly figured out why. My relationship with God had gotten in the way of me enjoying sex the way many of my friends talked about it. Because I had accepted His son Jesus into my life, He was there that day and I soon found out that He would be there every day thereafter. And as great as it was to have God watching over me daily, the last person I wanted to see or hear from in the middle of sex was Him!

As you might have figured out by now, I grew up in the church. My parents made me go every Sunday morning and Wednesday night. The only way I got out of going to church was if I was really sick, otherwise, I was there weekly. And so, from an early age, I knew that God wanted Christians to wait until they were married to have sex. Being a Christian, that meant me too. However, if I'm honest, I wasn't really sure **why** He wanted us to wait. No one really ever answered that question for me. As a result, I found living up to this expectation very difficult. The truth is, I wanted to have sex and even though I knew what God said, I was determined to test the limits of what was possible in order to fit in and be popular with friends.

In high school, opportunities to be alone with girls were pretty limited given that my parents were both teachers and always at home (*So annoying!*). This kept me out of trouble for the most part, but it didn't stop me from looking at nude magazines, watching X-rated films on Cinemax, or putting my hands in the pants and shirts of girls whenever we'd go out (movies, house parties, etc.) or even at school when no one was looking. When I would do these things, I knew I wasn't supposed to, but I felt like I deserved to have some fun. Why? No real reason other than everyone else was doing it (or at least talking about doing it), so why couldn't I? I didn't want to be known as a "Jesus freak" or a "Holy Roller," so I ignored what I knew God expected of me.

This pattern of doing what I wasn't supposed to do because everyone else was doing it continued throughout college. With my parents out of the picture, I finally had obtained the freedom necessary for me to graduate from "hand in pants" of girls to having sex with them. College gave me the chance to do whatever with whomever, however and whenever I wanted to. I was in a fraternity and numerous other organizations, which led to me being fairly popular on campus. With the number of female students largely outnumbering the number of male students, I had ample opportunity to continually ignore God's will for my life. And I did. However, just as I had experienced the very first time I had sex, many times I would find myself feeling guilty and shameful for what I had done. **God wouldn't leave me alone. He just wouldn't let me enjoy it.** But, that didn't stop me. Like a hardhead, I continued to have sex in hopes that the feelings of guilt and shame would eventually go away. They didn't. In fact, I started to notice that the more I tried to ignore God, the more difficult life became. My girlfriend and I stopped getting along. My friends were getting on my nerves. My job was no longer fun. Before long, I realized that I wasn't happy anymore. I was just going through the motions. It seemed that everything I put my hands on either broke or fell apart. I was confused. I had always thought that sex would make me happy. But, it didn't. Eventually, things got even worse. I was on the verge of going broke and losing all of my money. I hated my job and thought about quitting every day. My parents could not help me. My friends couldn't. Not even my pastor. No one could help me. And so, what did I do? I prayed to God for help.

It was in that prayer time with God that I came to realize He was calling me to a different standard of life. He wanted me to submit to Him and commit to a life of celibacy until marriage. He wanted me to stop disobeying Him. He wanted me to stop ignoring Him. He wanted me to trust Him with my life. No more sex. No more groping or fondling. No more treating women as objects. No more trying to be like everyone else just to fit in. It was time for me to become my own man. To do this, I would have to make some big changes in my life, but what did I have to lose? I needed help and after all, sex was not helping, but hurting me.

When I first started out with the whole "no sex until marriage thing," I had no idea what to do or how to do it. I made plenty of mistakes along the way, but because I was **willing** to try, God gave me answers where there were questions and strength where there was weakness. It wasn't easy, but with Him it was possible. And you know what happened? As soon as I started to focus on Him, my problems all began to work themselves out. My finances got better and I was no longer on the verge of being broke. My job situation improved and I found something that I enjoyed doing. I even found a young lady that I enjoyed spending time with. God, as He always does, worked it out. My life has never been the same. It was the best decision I could have made for my life!

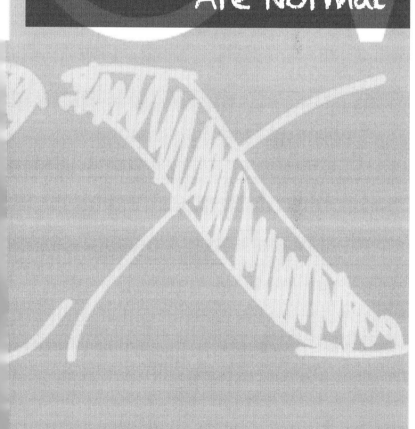

#1: Your Desires Are Normal

et's be honest. Girls, you are going to like boys. Nothing I or anyone else can do or say will change that. And fellas, you are going to like girls. This is a fact. It's normal! And you know what else is normal? You are going to be attracted to them, which will cause you to have sexual thoughts, desires, and urges in response to these feelings. Why? Because God made us that way! So, don't let anyone tell you that you are crazy, or weird, or out of control because you experience these things. They are normal responses to physical attraction. You see, it's not the fact that you have them that is the problem. Everybody has them! Everybody. Mom, dad, brother, sister, pastor, teacher...everybody. So again, it's not having these desires that's the problem. No, the problem is in how you handle these desires when you do have them. What do you do when you see a girl you're attracted to? What do you do when you and the boy you like are all alone in the back of the movie theater? In these situations and all others, **the key is to practice self-control.**

The Bible tells us in 1 *Thessalonians 4:3-5,*

> *"It is God's will that you should be sanctified: that you should avoid sexual immorality;* **that each of you should learn to control his own body in a way that is holy and honorable,** *not in passionate lust like the heathen, who do not know God."*

So, you may be thinking to yourself right now, "what does self-control look like?" Ultimately, it looks like acknowledging that your desires are real, but not allowing them to control you (self-control). Here are a few examples:

- It looks like going to the movies with the boy or girl you are attracted to and keeping your hands to yourself.

- It looks like going to prom with that boy or girl you've been feeling all year long, having a good

---

Notes:
Sanctified – To be purified or free of sin.
Sexual Immorality – Sexual interaction outside of God's original intent (e.g. fornication: outside of marriage, homosexuality: with same sex, adultery: with a married person, pornography: visual stimulation (magazines, internet, DVDs, etc.) masturbation: self-pleasure, groping/fondling: inappropriate, sexually motivated touching of another).
Lust – an intense desire or craving, typically referring to sex.
Heathen – strange, uncivilized.

time with them, and ending the night without crossing the line.

■ It looks like seeing the girl you think is fine walking down the hallway at school, admiring her beauty, but not reaching out to grab at her breasts or butt.

■ It looks like telling the boy you think is sexy "no" when he starts to rub on your body and kiss on your neck, even though you really want him to.

You have total control over your body and it cannot do what you do not allow it to do. The fact is, you will have desires...and to have them is normal. God isn't upset with you for having these desires. He expects it. After all, He made you. However, though He isn't upset with you for being attracted to the opposite sex and as a result, having sexual thoughts, desires, and urges, He does expect you to practice self-control.

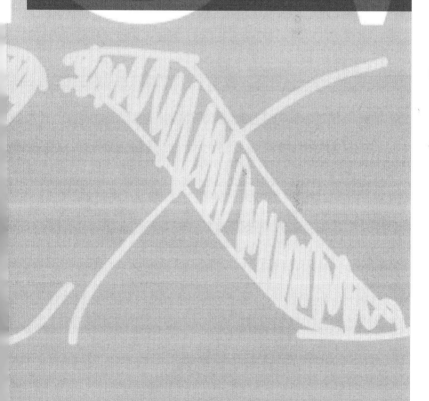

#2: Everyone is *NOT* Doing It

Here's the thing. I'm sure you're hearing all kinds of stories from your friends right now. They are telling you what they did, who they did it with, and even where they did it. And you know what? Some of them are probably telling the truth. That's the reality you live in; a reality where many of your friends are (or will be) doing the exact same things that your parents, church leaders, and teachers are telling you not to do. For every person that tells you not to have sex and wait until marriage, there's at least one friend out there who appears to be enjoying it and can't wait to tell you about it. And if I had to guess (because I remember how I felt), I'm sure this annoys and frustrates you. It makes you feel like you're missing out on something. It makes you feel like your parents, church leaders, and teachers have no idea what they are talking about. But, before you let it get to you, you want to know something interesting? A lot of what you are hearing is a lie.

Everyone is not doing it. Though it may sound like it, everyone is not having sex. In fact, the statistics say that less than half of all teenagers have had sex.[1]   Now, does that sound like everyone? No, it sounds like if you're "fleeing from sexual immorality" and waiting until you're married, you are not the only one by a long shot. Look at it this way. If you are in a room with 10 of your friends (or classmates), there's a good chance that at least 6 of them have never had sex. That's right, 6 out of 10 of them are probably virgins. So, while waiting may seem like the uncool thing to do, more of your friends are waiting than they would admit to you. I heard a quote somewhere a long time ago that says, ***"Believe none of what you hear and only half of what you see."*** When it comes to your friends and classmates, and who's doing what with whom, this quote definitely holds true. So, don't allow what you think others are doing, even if they've told you so, to influence what you do. ***Chances are, they are lying just to impress you.*** Don't fall for it! No matter what you hear, everyone is not doing it.

---

[1] http://thechart.blogs.cnn.com/2010/06/02/teens-having-sex-numbers-staying-steady/

#3a: If He Really Likes You, He Will Wait

Ladies, do you want to be married one day? Did you know that when it comes time to get married, most men look for women with the *lowest* number of sexual partners? In fact, **they prefer virgins.** *(Crazy, right? Especially considering how much they act like they don't value virginity when they're boys.)* They don't want the ones who have been 'getting it in' since high school and are 'easy'. While today, they might say they like the "freaks" or even post pictures of them on Instagram® (or any other social media outlet), those aren't the ones they'll eventually "wife up." See, when it comes time to settle down, they want the type of woman who has shown enough respect for herself to not let just any and everybody "see what she's working with." They want the type of woman who has practiced self-control with her desires. They want the type of woman who's been holding sacred her 'goodies' for the day she weds that special someone, her husband! So, don't fall for it when a boy tells you, "I *really* like you, but I *'need'* sex." If he *really* likes you, and plans to be with you longer than the time it takes to have sex with you, he'll be more than willing to wait. Plain. And. Simple.

But, what if I've already had sex? Does that mean that no man will ever want me to be his wife? Absolutely not! Many of us have made mistakes. I did. My wife did. But even in those mistakes, God is so loving that if we go to Him and ask for forgiveness, He gives us another chance. You get a chance to turn over a new leaf! A chance to start over. So, if you've already had sex, go to God right now and ask for forgiveness. Once you do this, He will make you as good as new for your future mate! For the Bible tells us in 1 John 1:9,

> *"If we confess our sins, **He is faithful and just to forgive us our sins** and to cleanse us from all un-righteousness."*

What does asking God for forgiveness look like? Here's an example prayer that you can use in this situation:

Notes:
Confess – to admit the truth.
Unrighteousness – all sinful behavior/nature.

Dear Lord,

I come to you now to ask for forgiveness for my sins. I know that the Bible says that I should wait until marriage to have sex, but I messed up. Please forgive me, Lord. From this day forward, I will do my best to please you and wait until I marry my husband to have sex. Thank you for giving me another chance. In Jesus' name I pray, Amen.

***

Before we move on, there is one other thing I want to share with you that is important for you to know as you are faced with the decision to have or not to have sex in the years to come. Your body is not your own. It is God's. And He paid a great price for you (He sacrificed His Son, Jesus, just so that you could be saved!). Not only that, but He made you for His purposes. He has a plan for your life! How awesome is that?! You're not here by accident. There is something that only you can do and that's why God has given you the life you have! As a result of these things, because your body is His and you're here on purpose, you have to treat your body with care.

Take a quick look at what the Bible says in **1 Corinthians 6:19-20,**

> " *Do you not know that your bodies are temples of the Holy Spirit, who is in you, whom you have received from God? You are not your own; you were* **bought at a price.** *Therefore honor God with your bodies.*"

Here, the Bible tells us that our bodies are temples of the Holy Spirit, which means God lives within us. He lives inside of you. In those moments, when it seems like you're all alone, He's there. When you find yourself enjoying the feeling of your boyfriend's hand sliding up your skirt or rubbing your breasts, God is there to help you resist. All you have to do is pray to Him and He will help you. It's much easier to flee if you call out to God *before* the clothes come off than trying to call on Him in the heat of the moment. What do you say when you call out to Him? Just be honest. It can be as simple as, *"God, I need your help right now to flee from sexual immorality."*

Notes:
"Bought At A Price" – This phrase references Jesus' death as the ransom for your salvation. The price for your life was paid by God with the blood of Jesus Christ.

Try praying that prayer next time and watch God come to your rescue.

#3b: If She Really Likes You She Will Respect Your Decision To Wait

Fellas, do you want women to respect you? Well, it may not seem like it right now, but if you continue to make choices based on God's will for your life, you will have more swag than you could ever imagine (And I know you have swag right now!). See, women love men who are willing to stand strong on their faith. These days, unfortunately, there are a lot of men who say they love the Lord, but don't mean it. They say all the right things to get a woman's attention, but then when the woman finds out they weren't serious, they leave them. As a result, women are fed up with playing games and so, when they find a man who's serious about his relationship with Christ... they (all of them...lol) cling to him.

I saw this come true in my own life. When I decided to take a stance for God and be celibate until marriage, at first I thought God was playing a joke on me. I would meet girls and as soon as I would tell them that I was waiting until marriage, their faces would turn up. Not before long, I stopped hearing from them. They didn't respect my decision to wait. And if I'm honest, I'll admit that I was initially frustrated because I thought that I'd end up being "lame" and never find a girl. I was like, "God, are you serious?!"

But then, things changed.

As I continued to obey God and live the way He wanted me to, I started to meet girls that were not only FINE, but also that respected my decision to wait! I was surprised, but it just proved to me that doing things God's way does pay off. Today, it may seem like remaining sexually pure and honoring God's standards are the 'uncool' things to do. But, trust me, if you do, you will find that it's one of the coolest and smartest things you could ever do. Meeting girls will not be a problem.

But, what if I've already had sex? Does that mean that no woman will ever respect me? **Absolutely not!** Many of us have made mistakes. I sure enough did. But even in those mistakes, God is so loving that if we go to Him and ask for forgiveness, He gives us another chance. You get a chance to turn over a new leaf! A chance to start over. So, if you've already had sex, go to God right now and ask for forgiveness. Once you do this, He will make sure that you are respected by women as you work to honor Him in your life by fleeing from sexual immorality and waiting until marriage to have sex. For the Bible tells us in **1 John 1:9,**

> *"If we confess our sins, He is faithful and just to forgive us our sins and to cleanse us from all unrighteousness."*

What does asking for forgiveness look like? Here is an example prayer that you can use if you are in this situation:

Dear Lord,

I come to you now to ask for forgiveness for my sins. I know that the Bible says that I should wait until marriage to have sex, but I messed up. Please forgive me, Lord. From this day forward, I will do my best to please you and wait until I marry my wife to have sex. Thank you for giving me another chance. In Jesus' name I pray, Amen.

***

Notes:
Confess – to admit the truth.
Unrighteousness – all sinful behavior/nature.

Before we move on, there is one other thing I want to share with you that is important for you to know as you are faced with the decision to have or not to have sex in the years to come. Your body is not your own. And it doesn't belong to the girl you like either. It is God's and He paid a great price for you (He sacrificed His Son, Jesus, just so that you could be saved!). Not only that, but He made you for His purposes. He has a plan for your life! How awesome is that?! You're not here by accident. There is something that only you can do and that's why God has given you the life you have! As a result of these things, because your body is His and you're here on purpose, you have to treat your body with care.

Take a quick look at what the Bible says in **1 Corinthians 6:19-20,**

> "*Do you not know that your bodies are temples of the Holy Spirit, who is in you, whom you have received from God? You are not your own; you were* **bought at a price. *Therefore honor God with your bodies.***"

Notes:
"Bought At A Price" – This phrase references Jesus' death as the ransom for your salvation. The price for your life was paid by God with the blood of Jesus Christ.

Here, the Bible tells us that our bodies are temples of the Holy Spirit, which means God lives within us. He lives inside of you. In those moments, when it seems like you're all alone, He's there. When you find yourself enjoying the way your girlfriend's breasts feel in your hands or the way it feels when she is grinding in your lap, God is there to help you resist. All you have to do is pray to Him and He will help you. It's much easier to flee if you call out to God *before* the clothes come off than trying to call on Him in the heat of the moment. What do you say when you call out to Him? Just be honest. It can be as simple as, *"God, I need your help right now to flee from sexual immorality."* Try praying that prayer next time and watch God come to your rescue.

#4: God Wants You To Wait To Protect You

You know your parents love you, right? Great. Then, let me ask you a quick question. *What is their #1 priority in life as it relates to you?* To protect you! At the end of the day, your parents will do anything...anything to protect you! Even when they know that protecting you will make them the least favorite person in your world, they will still, without hesitation, do it. (I know, I know... this "protecting stuff" can get on your nerves sometimes... LOL!)

Well, God is the same way! He didn't tell us to remain sexually pure and wait until marriage because He wanted to be corny and punish us. He set these standards because He was (and is) fully aware of the damage that **sexual immorality** can do to you. And so, He wants, just like your parents, to protect you; protect you from the *physical, emotional, and spiritual consequences* of sexual immorality. As I mentioned earlier, He has plans for your life. You are not an accident. Your life has purpose and God needs you to be in the best physical, emotional, and spiritual state in order to accomplish all He has for you! Those dreams you have? He gave them to you and ultimately, He's counting on you to do only what you can do to help Him fulfill His plans for this world. So, let's take a look at what God's protecting you from and explore the consequences that can come from making the decision to go against His will.

PHYSICAL

As you well know, there are many physical consequences to sexual immorality. And while the emotional and spiritual may not be visible to others, the physical consequences usually show up pretty clear via **HIV/AIDs and other Sexually Transmitted Diseases (STDs).** Approximately 50% of all new STD's contracted each year are among teenagers and young adults.[2] To put it another way, **if there are 500 people in your school, there is a good chance that 250 of them already have or will contract an STD before graduating**. So, whether you know it or not, it is highly likely that you will or already

[2]*http://www.cdc.gov/HealthyYouth/sexualbehaviors/*

know someone who has an STD. Is that surprising to you?

I remember when I started having sex, I was most afraid of the physical consequences. Even though I used condoms the majority of the time, I was still afraid that with my luck, one would break and I would either catch something that couldn't be cured (Herpes, HPV, HIV) or get a girl pregnant.[3] And you know what the worst part was? The much dreaded STD/HIV tests. Though I didn't want to get tested, I knew I had to because there was nothing worse than having something and not knowing it. I remember getting those tests like it was yesterday. I would lose my appetite and feel sick to my stomach as I waited for the results. I would be a nervous wreck. It was one of the most stressful experiences ever and I felt like a complete idiot because it was my fault. There was no one else to blame. It was me who made the decision to have sex and if I caught something in the act, well...I would have to deal with it. But, if I would have just followed God's standard, I wouldn't have had to go through it...but I didn't, and as a result, I had to go through it.

[3]http://www.cdc.gov/std/default.htm

Thankfully, by the grace of God, I never got anyone pregnant or contracted an STD. But, not all of my friends were that blessed. I know many people who got someone/became pregnant and plenty more who contracted an STD all while embracing, instead of fleeing, sexual immorality. If you were to ask them in private, "Was it worth it?" I know that most of them would tell you, "No!" Now, that doesn't mean that their lives were doomed from that point forward, it just means that because of the consequences of their decisions, their lives have been more difficult than they had to be.

What's worse? To get someone/become pregnant or to contract an incurable STD? You might be thinking get someone/become pregnant because there's no hiding from that, whereas, if you contracted an incurable STD no one else has to know. And if that were your line of thinking, then you would be right. No one else has to know, but you would know. And if you decide to get married one day...your husband-to-be or wife-to-be will know (or find out the hard way). And they will have to make a decision about whether or not they are willing to marry you knowing that you have an incurable STD. Now, that's a tough decision. Think about that. Your dream of being with Mr. or Mrs. Right, raising 2 kids, and living in The Hamptons happily-ever-after could be ruined all because of an STD you contracted as a teenager. Wow. But, thankfully, this dream doesn't have to be ruined if you just follow God's standards and flee from sexual immorality! Following Him is the best contraception available and it is sure to keep you baby and STD-free. He wants to protect you from these physical consequences. **HE HAS YOUR BACK!** You just have to follow Him.

EMOTIONAL

What do you think some of the emotional consequences of sexual immorality are? Well, first, you should know that the pursuit of sex is very time-consuming. It takes time away from activities that you could be doing to help you achieve your dreams. It could quite easily become the thing that stands between you and success. As you might imagine, not living up to your potential or reaching the level of success you dream about would be very disappointing. Second, all those text messages, social media posts (Facebook, Twitter, Instagram, YouTube, Vine, etc.), and phone conversations late into the night take a ton of emotional energy. You spend a ton of time thinking of cute or clever things to say, post, or record in hopes that the person you are feeling will see it and respond. And then, you wait around anxiously for their response. Whether it is a simple "like" or "comment," when they finally respond, you feel something. Maybe they like you? Maybe you are special? And now that they "like you," you continue to try to impress them and if successful, the two of you will eventually form a relationship. Before you know it, you feel like you know them well enough to have sex with them. And once you do, the door to emotional pain becomes wide open. How so? Glad you asked.

Well, let's say that you end up having sex with them. And this 'special someone' who you had sex with either "cheats" on you (and has sex with someone else) or drops you like a bad habit (stops returning your texts, responding to your posts, or calling you back). How would you feel if this happens? Hurt? Depressed? Angry? That's how I felt. I remember getting cheated on in high school and the embarrassment I felt, the anger I had when I finally found out. I remember getting played in college (multiple times) and how depressed I was after "she" wouldn't even call me back (We didn't have Facebook or Instagram back then, so I didn't have to worry about her not "liking" or "commenting" on my posts...lol). While I felt my emotions were justified, the reality is that they only served to distract me from more important things in my life. They kept me from enjoying life the way that God wanted me to because I was so focused on what "she" had done to me that I couldn't think about anything else. When I look back over my experiences, I realize it wasn't worth it. Each time I engaged in sexual immorality, I gave the other person a piece of myself that I never got back. That's why it hurt when I got cheated on. That's why it was painful when I got played. And do you want to know who the only person was that ever gave me back what I gave to them? My wife...and once I saw that, I realized that God was trying to protect me from the emotional consequences of sexual immorality all those times before.

So, take it from me, your best bet to protect yourself emotionally is to stay away from sexual immorality so you don't find yourself hurt, depressed, or angry. It's more to life than those three emotions. When you are hurt, depressed or angry, it is very difficult to do well in school, focus on sports, and enjoy hanging out with your friends. Everything will annoy you and you will end up not wanting to be around anyone. Now, does that sound like fun?

No, of course not! So, trust me when I tell you, God wants you to wait to protect you. You will have *plenty* of time to deal with life's troubles, so no point in rushing things and forcing yourself to deal with them this early.

SPIRITUAL

At this point, I'm sure you are clear on God's will for you as it relates to sex (and sexual immorality). Well, one of the things we haven't touched on yet are the spiritual consequences of doing the opposite of what God wants. When you go against God's will for your life, there's usually some spiritual baggage that comes with it (Just imagine putting a 50-lb duffle bag on your back for a 10 mile jog. It will be much more difficult to jog 10 miles with the duffle bag on than without, right?). You may find yourself feeling guilty and not wanting to go to church for fear of someone finding out what you did. Or, you might not want to pray anymore because you think God's mad at you. When these two things happen, what you end up doing is **damaging the relationship you have with God.** It's not because He has changed, it's because you have. Through your actions, you're no longer as open with Him and that causes the relationship to breakdown. But, just like your parents, God wants you to always feel like you can talk to Him. And though it's hard when you know He's going to be disappointed, you have to continue to go to Him. He's the only one who can help you do better next time. The goal is always to go to Him with everything, however, when we make wrong choices we allow our guilt and shame to get in the way of our relationship with God. So, as I've said earlier in this book, flee from sexual immorality. In doing so, you ensure that you keep the lines of communication between you and God open. **Don't let sex come between you and God!**

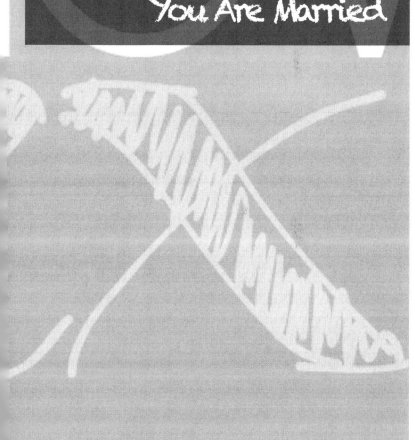

#5: It's Better When You Are Married

The 5th and final thing that every teen should know about sex is, "It's better when you're married!" I'll get to that in a second, but I bet right now you're thinking to yourself, "what good does that do me?" That's a great question. Did you know that every relationship decision you make from this day forward will have an impact on your marriage one day? And did you know that every sexual experience you have until you get married adds to your "sexual memory bank?" Sure, marriage for you might be 15-20 years from now, but know that you are making important choices today (and for the next 15-20 years) that will impact your future marriage.

For example, one of the things I didn't understand until I got married was this idea of a "sexual memory bank." Do you know what that is? Well, a sexual memory bank is where all the sexual encounters you've had with other people are stored in your brain. And while that might sound cool right now, it becomes very uncool when you're ready to get married. You see, the problem when you get married, when you have finally settled down with the one for you, is that those memories from all the other people are still there! Fellas, that girl from your sophomore year in high school who really put it on you? Yeah, she's there in the memory bank. Or, ladies, the college guy that you met your junior year who was the "best you ever had." Yup, he's there in there, too. These memories won't go away and they can become a huge problem in a marriage. Why? Well, fellas, if you're wife doesn't do what the girl from your sophomore year in high school did, how will you handle that? Will you still love her? Ladies, what if your husband isn't as good as the "college guy?" What will you do? Will you tell him? Here's where some would say, "That's why you gotta test drive the car before you buy it." Or in other words, "That's why you have to have sex with someone before you marry them." But, that doesn't solve the problem. The problem exists because you've embraced sexual immorality, and not fled from it, for a number of years and you now have the memories to live with. And when you get up there at the altar to say your vows with the one you love, you bring with you all of those experiences along too. If you've had 12 sexual partners, then on your wedding day it's really like you plus

them (13 people in all) are all marrying your husband/
wife. So, the fewer sexual experiences you create and add
to your "sexual memory bank," the better sex will be inside of marriage for you.

Now, back to the main point I wanted to hit on
with this section. The reason that it (sex) is better when
you're married is because **when you're married, you're
free.** You're free from the physical, emotional, and spiritual consequences that come with having sex outside
of God's intended purpose! When you're married, **God
honors it and looks for you and your spouse to do it...
often!** In fact, it's against His will for you "not to do it"
unless you agree to. *Imagine that!* God wants you to enjoy sex and all that comes with it! *So, no matter how
good people tell you it is outside of marriage, I stand
here as someone who's married to let you know that
it gets better...but only when you're married.*

You know the other reason it's better when you're
married? Because when you're not spending all of your
time dealing with the physical, emotional, and spiritual
drama from doing it outside God's will, you will find that
you will have more time to pursue your dreams. You will
have more time to become the man or woman that God

wants you to be. You can focus on becoming great while others are focused on sex. And when the time comes, **God will honor your commitment and pair you up with someone else just as awesome as you.** So, don't worry about what "everyone" else says they're doing or the folks that mock you because of what you're doing. All you have to do is worry about what God thinks and if you honor Him...He'll think you're pretty awesome! And because of that, once you're married you'll find out just how awesome He thinks you are!

The Bible tells us in G*alatians* **6:9,**

> *"Let us not become weary in doing good, **for at the proper time** we will reap a harvest if we do not give up."*

In other words, don't give up on God and He won't give up on you! IT IS WORTH THE WAIT!

Notes:
"Reap" – This word means "to collect" as in pick up the good crop that has grown during the season.
"Harvest" – This term is used to an agricultural expression that speaks to the "fruit" that is born from hard work of the farmer in the field.

Now What?

So, you've made it to the end. Congratulations! But, wait...what do you do now? You may be thinking to yourself, "If I'm not having sex or pursuing sex, what am I supposed to do?" Glad you asked! Below are a few suggestions of things you can do:

1. Pursue academic excellence

Focus on your schoolwork. Give it everything you've got to get straight A's. Better grades equal better opportunities. Better opportunities equal more money. And who doesn't like more money?

2. Get a hobby

What is it that you like doing? What is it that you're really interested in? Reading? Riding your bike? Collecting baseball cards? Baking? Maybe you don't know. If you don't, that's okay because you can use this time to figure it out. As you get older, having a hobby will come in handy because it will help you relax when you get stressed out or frustrated with life.

3. Perfect your "craft" (aka what you're naturally good at)

How many hours do you think LeBron James practiced his jump shot before he made it to the NBA? How much time do you think Beyonce spent working on her dance moves or working on her vocals before Destiny's Child blew up? Excellence isn't born overnight! It comes through sacrifice and countless hours of practice. So, get to it! Your greatness is waiting on you!

4. Get a mentor

Do you know what a mentor is? A mentor is someone who is willing to guide you in life, hold you accountable to your goals, and help you make the right choices. It could be a family member that you trust. A coach. A teacher. A guidance counselor. A pastor. It can be anyone who you have witnessed make the right choices in their life and as a result, you respect who they are and look up to them.

Over the next week or so, think about who in your life could be your mentor. Once you identify who it is, go to them (in person) and ask them if they would be willing to be your mentor.

5. Get involved in the community

You probably think you're too young for this. But, that's not true. There are kids right now that look up to you. They follow your every move and mimic your every action. One of the greatest things you can do in life is to help others. Shifting your energy and focus from sex to helping others is one sure way to make a difference in this world. Ask your teachers if you can tutor someone in a grade below you. Ask your parents if you can volunteer at the YMCA. Use this time wisely and you will be surprised at how much you will enjoy it.

6. Grow in your relationship with God

What better way to show God that you love Him than to obey Him?! Now that you've committed to living for Him in this area of your life, spend time with Him to grow even closer to Him. Read your Bible. Go to church. Pray. All of these things will help you come to know Him better. He opens doors for those He knows! And He protects those who He has a relationship with!

These are just a few things that you can do with the time you've gained back by committing to abstinence until marriage, but there are many more. If you need some other suggestions or want to get some advice, just email me at 5ThingsAboutSex@gmail.com.

IMPORTANT POINT

The first step to establishing a relationship with God is to accept His Son Jesus Christ as your Lord and personal Savior. The Bible tells us in Romans 10:9, that *"If you declare with your mouth, "Jesus is Lord," and believe in your heart that God raised him from the dead, you will be saved."* Salvation is available to you RIGHT NOW if you "declare with your mouth that Jesus is Lord" and believe in your heart that God raised Him from the dead.

Conclusion

That's it! My hope is that you've enjoyed this book, but more importantly, I hope you have learned some new things about sex. The reality is that you will be faced with many decisions about sex in the days ahead. Some of you may have already had to make tough decisions and if you haven't, those decision points are on the way. So, when you have to make those decisions, be sure to remember:

1. **Your desires are normal.** *(Don't beat yourself up for feeling how you feel.)*

2. **Everyone is NOT doing it!** *(Don't let others make you do something you don't want to do.)*

3. **If he really likes you, he'll wait.** *(If he won't wait, he's not the one for you.)*

3. **If she really likes you, she'll respect your decision to wait.** *(Don't worry...if she won't respect your decision to wait, someone else will.)*

4. **God wants you to wait to protect you.** *(God loves you and wants nothing more than for you to live a happy life!)*

5. **It is better when you're married!** *(Waiting will make your wedding night extra special!)*

You have your whole life in front of you and by making the right decisions about sex from this day forward, you will give yourself the best opportunity to have a healthy and successful life!

Acknowledgements

I want to send a special shout out to the following Teen Reviewers who provided me with excellent feedback during the creation of this book! Without their input, The **5 Things Every Teen Should Know About Sex** would not have been possible!

Mikaela Quick

JaLesa Byes

Marcus Tatum

Jordan Rabb

Cedric Brazille

Zemi Jacob

Aside from these awesome teenagers, I want to thank God for giving me a vision many years ago that has now become a book! I thank Him for entrusting me with a message for His people and I pray that this book fulfills His will. Also, I would like to thank my beautiful wife who endured many hours of me talking about this book...

LOL! Thanks 'Babe' for reading the book twice, providing a female opinion, and giving me extremely valuable feedback! You continue to amaze me and I am thankful for the love that we share as it grows each and every day! And last, but certainly not least, I want to thank my boys Jaha Howard, Justin Smith, and Conrod Kelly for reading the first draft and providing me with invaluable insight and feedback. Thanks for keeping me honest and challenging me in the writing process!

About the Author

bony & Essence Magazine featured author, Armond Mosley, is a sought after speaker who is passionate about helping youth realize their potential and achieve their dreams. Through seminars and workshops, Armond partners with organizations (educational, faith-based, civic) to provide their youth with practical and actionable advice to address the real challenges that come with being young in today's society. Some of his signature seminar/workshop offerings are: ***Success Is A Choice, The 5 Things Every Teen Should Know About Sex, and Never Accept Less Than Your Best.***

Born in Huntsville, AL, Armond is a graduate of Howard University (BS. ChE '03) and Temple University (MBA '10). He now resides in the suburbs of Philadelphia with his wife Nneka. Currently, Armond is actively promoting his first book, ***Rededication: A Story of Sex, Repentance and Restoration*** and working on his third book, which will deal with relationships, to be released in the Spring of 2014. In his spare time, Armond enjoys reading, traveling, watching sports, and spending time with family and friends.

To learn more about Armond, visit his website at **www.armondmosley.com** or follow him on Social Media (Twitter, Facebook, Instagram) at **@iammosley**. For questions about booking Armond for a speaking engagement, email him at **5ThingsAboutSex@gmail.com**.